GW00716690

About Demos

Demos is a greenhouse for new ideas which can improve the quality of our lives. As an independent think tank, we aim to create an open resource of knowledge and learning that operates beyond traditional party politics.

We connect researchers, thinkers and practitioners to an international network of people changing politics. Our ideas regularly influence government policy, but we also work with companies, NGOs, colleges and professional bodies.

Demos knowledge is organised around five themes, which combine to create new perspectives. The themes are democracy, learning, enterprise, quality of life and global change.

But we also understand that thinking by itself is not enough. Demos has helped to initiate a number of practical projects which are delivering real social benefit through the redesign of public services.

We bring together people from a wide range of backgrounds to cross-fertilise ideas and experience. By working with Demos, our partners develop a sharper insight into the way ideas shape society. For Demos, the process is as important as the final product.

www.demos.co.uk

First published in 2004
© Demos
Some rights reserved – see copyright licence for details

ISBN 1 84180 126 7
Typeset by Land & Unwin, Bugbrooke
Printed by Hendy Banks, London

For further information and
subscription details please contact:

Demos
The Mezzanine
Elizabeth House
39 York Road
London SE1 7NQ

telephone: 0845 458 5949
email: hello@demos.co.uk
web: www.demos.co.uk

Creative Reading

Young people, reading and public libraries

John Holden

DEM⊙S

DEMⓒS

Contents

Acknowledgements

This report was made possible by the support of The Reading Agency. My sincere thanks go to Miranda McKearney, Debbie Hicks and Ruth Harrison who have been a consistent source of good ideas, support and assistance. I would also like to thank all those who were interviewed for the project and all of those who gave comments on work in progress, including Abigail Campbell, Jonathan Douglas, Mairie Gelling, Patsy Heap, Rebecca Hunter, Sue Jones, Charles Leadbeater, Gary McKeone, Neil McLelland, Chris Meade, Andrew Stevens, Sarah Wilkie, Sue Wilkinson and Alec Williams.

My thanks also go to my colleagues at Demos, in particular to Tom Bentley, Eddie Gibb, Robert Hewison, Masanari Koike, Charlie Tims, Bobby Webster and Shealagh Wright.

The people mentioned above provided help and assistance, but all errors and omissions remain my own.

John Holden
June 2004

Foreword

The debate about libraries rages. Are they failing or changing? The recent rise in visitor figures and the energy and innovation of their work with readers suggests the latter.

The debate needs to move to a new level, based on a better understanding of the twenty-first-century role that public libraries can play, not just on book issuing statistics. This role must have the encouragement of reading at its heart.

We are delighted to have commissioned this Demos paper about creativity, libraries and reading to move the debate on and are most grateful to the Department of Culture, Media and Sport for the support that has made this possible.

We hope the paper will focus attention on libraries as creative institutions and on the underplayed potential of their work with young readers. It is time for libraries to be much more fully recognised as part of the creative world, with an important role to play in the emerging creativity and cultural entitlement agenda.

The library service faces huge challenges, but is working in new ways to reach and inspire young readers. This work injects creativity into community in a big way, and deserves much greater attention. Its power to help achieve our national ambitions should not be under-estimated.

Miranda McKearney
Director, The Reading Agency

Preface

This report examines how reading and public libraries connect with the creative potential of young people. Consequently it has a broad range, looking at the interaction of institutions (for example, between schools and libraries), concepts (for example, between creativity and reading) and other factors (for example, the attitudes of young people), rather than examining any one aspect in depth. It is meant to be provocative and thought-provoking, and to raise questions for those involved to answer for themselves. I hope that it will be of interest to librarians, teachers, policy-makers, local authorities and school library services among others.

John Holden
Demos

Introduction

○ Creativity is widely accepted as a major driver of economic growth and prosperity. It is also important in terms of realising human potential. The importance of creativity in education is gaining currency.

○ Reading, though often perceived as passive and receptive, is a creative activity in itself, and frequently an important element in other creative processes.

○ Young people need to be equipped with high-level reading skills to get the most out of cultural and social life and to meet the challenges of the twenty-first-century job market. Research shows that life chances are improved by reading. We need to go beyond literacy so that young people enjoy reading and cultivate a range of reading abilities.

○ Public libraries already play a vital role in nurturing reading, but they are forgotten players in the creativity debate and their potential is vastly underrated.

○ Libraries themselves need to recognise that they are part of the creative world, and to understand more fully the role that they can play in helping young people to be creative.

○ Libraries can offer creative spaces, activities and programmes, but all libraries need to reach the standards of the best.

○ Harnessing the power of libraries to work with young people outside school, and forging better connections between schools and libraries are both needed in order to release young people's creativity.

We are boxed in by clichés when we start to think about reading. People 'curl up with a good book' or they 'have their noses in a book'. The quiet types are 'bookish' or 'bookworms'. Readers always seem to be on their own, self-absorbed and silent. From the odious Mr Casaubon in *Middlemarch* via Billy Bunter to the archivist in Polanski's *Chinatown*, those who spend their lives with books are depicted as antisocial, withdrawn and dull.

This study sets out to explode the myth that reading is a personal and essentially passive pursuit. It concentrates on looking at reading as a creative activity, and addresses how reading, assisted by public libraries and their links with schools, helps young people to become creative individuals. It argues that libraries, schools and the cultural sector, working individually and in partnership, can play an increasingly important role – both in helping the next generation to lead richer lives and by preparing them for their role in the creative economy.

Reading is our most popular cultural activity.

Fiction and non-fiction together are read in 90 per cent of the nation's households and book sales have risen by 30 per cent over the last four years.[1] Some of those will be reference or cookery books, rather than bought for reading, but the trend is undeniable. More importantly, reading is a vitally important gateway to economic, social and civic life. As the Department for Culture Media and Sport (DCMS) notes in *Framework for the Future*: 'People cannot be active or informed citizens unless they can read. Reading is a prerequisite for almost all cultural and social activities'.[2] Life chances are improved when you can read. Research from the Organisation for Economic Co-operation and Development (OECD) shows that a love of reading is more important for a child's educational success than their family's wealth or class[3], and in that sense reading can be a ticket out of deprivation.

But while basic literacy and the needs of the socially excluded are important, we must also be aware that reading is a vital skill throughout society. Most of us will change not just our jobs, but our careers and our leisure activities during our lives. The need for individual, regular re-invention is no longer confined to Madonna and Bowie but is already affecting vast numbers of people. High-level creative reading skills, coupled with an ability to navigate information sources and to synthesise experience into learning, now form part of the toolkit that young people need in order to get the most out of their lives.

1. Reading

> *What is reading then? The answer is not simple, as the act of reading is variable not absolute. In its most general modern definition, reading is of course the ability to make sense of written or printed symbols.*
>
> Steven Roger Fischer[4]

Reading has a history. It has changed from being an elite preserve to become, in the West at least, an almost universal capability. Philip Pullman recently referred in a speech to 'the greatest achievement of human culture, the democracy of reading', and his comment points to the fact that reading is not just personally liberating, it is politically important. Dictators and bigots often burn books as part of their efforts to suppress free thought.

Somewhere in the eighteenth century the act of

reading gradually became internalised. Boswell was amazed to find Johnson reading noiselessly to himself. Now we live with a view of reading as essentially passive, something that people do quietly by themselves, their own private and solitary concern. In public places, reading is an escape from one's surroundings.

Reading also has a future and that future may be more social. We now have mass reading, where children talk about their shared experience and interpretation of books just as avidly as they discuss the latest soaps. We have book clubs and reading groups, and public readings have been re-invented. Crossovers between different media, with TV and film promoting obscure texts into bestsellers, and screenplays turned into books, are an important cultural phenomenon.

What is going on when we read?

So what is going on when we read? Far from being an act of passive consumption, where the reader absorbs the writer's words like a sponge, reading in itself is a creative process. No two people read the same text in the same way. Everyone brings their own set of expectations, experiences and viewpoints; what occurs is a dialogue between reader and writer, what emerges is a changed person. We take what a writer gives us and we make it our own. We do not only gain knowledge from reading, we acquire emotional depth and subtlety of response. We can become more empathetic, and we can also heal ourselves: the therapeutic value of reading in hospitals is well established.

There are different levels of reading accomplishment. In the contemporary knowledge economy, multiple reading skills are needed. Basic literacy is not enough. Readers must be able to navigate different sources of knowledge, know where to go looking for what they need, and be able to analyse, interpret and synthesise. They need to be self-reflective and self-aware. Sometimes they have to scan texts to pick out nuggets of useful data, at other times they have to concentrate hard to uncover deep and complex meanings. The possession of these high-level critical reading abilities is not only useful for people in their working lives, but just as importantly it adds texture and depth to the whole of life, from social relationships to the enjoyment of culture. The question for most people today is not whether they can read, but how well they can read: 'A developmental view of reading permits us to picture the trajectory of our reading experience as a movement from unreflecting engagement to deliberate choice about the kind of readers we will be and the uses to which we will put our reading'.[5]

In this sense, then, reading is complex and it is creative: what we start with is not what we end with. When people read they make words real, they put themselves in the places and situations that are described in the text, they play with meanings and act out scenes in their heads. This imaginative engagement is a creative endeavour. But does reading really fit with the ways that we think and talk about creativity? Are we stretching the language too far in using the phrase 'creative reading', when most people's notion of creativity is that it is something that takes place in an artistic or scientific context?

2. Creativity

One must be an inventor to read well.
Ralph Waldo Emerson[6]

In various interviews for this project, I repeatedly heard that 'Reading is not seen as being creative', and 'I think reading is creative, but most people don't. They think creative means theatre and painting'.

Creativity is a concept that is difficult to define. We have been struggling with it ever since Socrates' dialogue with Ion. The National Advisory Committee on Creative and Cultural Education (NACCCE) came up with the following definition: 'imaginative activity fashioned so as to produce outcomes that are both original and of value'.[7] This is a useful start but, like all previous and subsequent attempts, no one sentence can encompass all the subtleties and nuances of what we mean when we talk about creativity.

Later on we will look at how reading connects with aspects of creativity such as autonomy, risk-taking, stimulus and experimentation, and how libraries engage with some of the characteristics of creativity, but for now one nettle needs to be grasped. Reading is often seen as 'not creative' because it has no physical output. There is no product, no performance, nothing that the reader can point to and say 'There!' Our most deep-rooted and fundamental belief about creativity is that it is an act with a product. It goes back to the very beginnings of monotheistic religion when God created the earth. But the NACCCE definition carefully and helpfully uses the word 'outcome' instead of 'product' and while the act of reading may produce no physical outcome, it does produce an outcome of value – a changed person, with more knowledge or more emotional depth or both.

The most successful economies and societies

in the twenty-first century will be the creative ones. Creativity will make the difference – to businesses seeking a competitive edge, to societies looking for new ways to tackle issues and improve quality of life.[8]

More and more, creativity is being regarded as the engine of economic growth. The application of knowledge to make improvements in products, services and processes is seen as vital if we are to be a successful and thriving nation. Writers such as Tom Bentley, Richard Florida and Charles Leadbeater have demonstrated that an ever-increasing proportion of GDP is generated in the 'creative economy' and that it is growing faster than the rest of the economy. Florida has further shown that, in the US, those people who work in the creative economy, those he calls 'the creative class', are earning more than others and taking a greater share of the overall cake. So, although the advantages that come with creativity are a driving force of prosperity, those that lack them are falling further and further behind. In this way, while creativity is producing richer individuals – in every sense – and a growing economy, it may also be contributing to increased inequality.

Not surprisingly, for all of these reasons – economic, social and quality of life – creativity is high on the agenda in policy circles and government. The NACCCE report identified a set of economic, technological, social and personal challenges faced by young people and called for 'a much stronger emphasis on creative and cultural education'.[9]

This climate of interest in creativity is reflected in ministerial pronouncements, such as Charles Clarke's statement that 'Creativity isn't an add-on. It must form a vital and integral part of every child's experience at school'.[10] New initiatives including Creative Partnerships, the National Endowment for Science Technology and the Arts (NESTA), the Museums and Galleries Education Programme (MGEP) and the New Opportunities Fund (NOF) all reflect an interest in finding out more about how young people can become more creative and how they can be equipped to lead fulfilling lives in the twenty-first century.

Public libraries also have an important role to play in the creativity agenda, They have long been seen as repositories of knowledge and places of learning, but there is much new work going on in terms of programmes, organisational innovation and ways of working in partnership. What exactly are they doing, and could they do more? In what ways can they help young people to become creative thinkers and doers?

3. Creativity, reading and public libraries

The reason for believing that library services do indeed have a future is simple. Now, and for the foreseeable future, people will need to upgrade their skills or learn new ones many times in the course of their working – and even domestic and recreational – lives. Education will no longer be a once and for all operation at the outset of life, but a continuous process of adaptation, self-development and vocational re-skilling.

Building Futures[11]

In order to understand the role of public libraries in nurturing creativity we need to work with a conceptual framework that untangles creativity into a number of elements that form recognisable features of the creative process. We need a way of thinking and talking about creativity that will help libraries to appreciate their role and understand where they can make beneficial changes.

Creativity is in some ways mysterious, and it is highly individual – one person can use a set of contexts and inputs to produce something that is new, while another is left uninterested and unmoved – but this element of mystery should not blind us to what we do know. Certain things like stimulation, enjoyment, experimentation and peer group acceptance help to promote creativity. Equally repetition, risk-aversion and peer negativity tend to destroy it.

We understand that some places provide environments that are more conducive to creative thought than others. Individual buildings sometimes have a *genius loci* that both reflects and promotes an organisational culture of creativity. Certain areas of cities develop 'creative clusters' where a subtle blend of competition and cooperation between the elements maintains a climate of invention and innovation. Public libraries should be part of such creative clusters.

These elements – experiences, attitudes, skills, environment and place – work together to provide a complex mix that produces a creative individual – someone with the right ingredients of confidence, originality, persistence, knowledge and motivation.

What follows is an attempt to 'map' public libraries against creativity by looking at aspects of the creative process under the broad headings of cognition, knowledge, attitudes and motivation. In other words, how do libraries help people to think and act differently in order to produce new outcomes?

Cognition

The starting point for the creative process is the ability not to solve a problem but to *define* a problem. It begins with asking questions. As Ofsted emphasises: 'In successful teaching for creativity, teachers…provide pupils with challenges where there is no clear-cut solution'.[12] At the heart of this mental process is curiosity, a desire to find out how to do something in a different way, and libraries are *par excellence* places to satisfy curiosity. But in the creative process satisfying curiosity on one matter simply leads to more questions. Curiosity stimulates a flow of interest, connecting one thing with another.[13]

One of the most interesting things about reading and the use of libraries is their ability to connect one piece of information or experience with another. Forging connections – making mental leaps between one thing and another – can be deep when reading the entire works of one author, or every book on a particular subject, and it can be broad – following a chain from works on canal boats to eighteenth-century history to classicism to Greek architecture, for example. The path of a reader is not a runway but more a hack through a forest, with individual twists and turns, entanglements and moments of surprise.

The crucial point here is that skilled readers relentlessly question the text. They scan bibliographies and indexes, put together what they know with what they are discovering, create new formations from their explorations, and look for ways to add to their knowledge and learning.

This 'ability to connect' is not confined to books. Many young people use a combination of reading, music, web searches and pictures to satisfy their curiosity and libraries can meet this need with their increasing range of resources across different media. A variety of media also helps to satisfy different young people's individual learning styles.

The writer on creativity and education Arthur Cropley identifies as one feature of creativity the readiness to be open to subconscious material.[14] We are all aware that many ideas occur when we appear to be 'coasting', and one interviewee for this project noted that ideas 'tend to pop into the mind' when reading. A random word or sentence can prompt original thought or the recognition of a connection.

Cropley also sees the mental capacity to abstract from the concrete as a feature of creativity. Taking general principles from particular occurrences and events is at the heart of reading, particularly reading fiction, where individual characters and their stories point to more general truths about the human condition. An ability to conceptualise and to discriminate between the general and the particular are both helped by reading.

Knowledge

In the creative process knowledge is applied in new ways to provide original solutions. Creativity does not occur in a vacuum, but always results from standing on the shoulders of our predecessors and adapting and changing existing knowledge. Public libraries are the richest repositories and stores of knowledge that we have – and they are free. As *Framework for the Future* says, 'libraries have a central role to play in ensuring everyone has access to the resources, information and knowledge that they need'.[15]

Knowledge content is accessible in libraries through books, periodicals, videos, CDs and online through the People's Network and Learndirect. There is no limit to the availability of the raw sum of human knowledge via libraries. But raw knowledge is in itself of little value. It needs to be contextualised, linked to other forms of knowledge, internalised and manipulated. Libraries offer multiple entry points into the world of knowledge for young people, and the guidance of librarians in encouraging connections is vital. The 'If you liked that, then you may like this' tactic adopted by internet booksellers was invented in libraries.

Libraries need to be adventurous in their approach to creating a variety of entry points to knowledge. They should all, for example, stock a range of teen magazines, and try to engage with places where young people are, rather than expecting young people to find them.

An important feature of knowledge in the context of creativity is the way that it acts as a stimulus to imagination, enquiry and curiosity. This stimulus is often helped by an element of randomness, which libraries can create in the way that they display and arrange some of their material. 'Creative browsing' – which is observable in bookshops as well as libraries – should be encouraged. Browsing the shelves is in fact the original model for web-surfing. There are many examples of how creative browsing can be stimulated, from Leeds public library displaying a range of books by their colour to Norwich public library having an express, bookshop-style choice of books for a speedy checkout.

Attitudes

Creative people display a set of attitudes that enables them to apply their knowledge in innovative ways. They tend to have a willingness to experiment. They accept a degree of risk and uncertainty that inevitably flows from originality. They also tend to be happy with complexity, and resist the pressure to close down possibilities in an attempt to simplify. They ask questions, and challenge the status quo and accepted ways of doing things.

In many cases these are also the characteristics of high-level critical reading. Confident readers will manifest all of these traits. It would be interesting to research the correlation between approaches to reading and creative thinking skills, but it would not be unreasonable to expect a virtuous circle between what the OECD calls 'the active and interactive role of the reader in finding meaning from written texts'[16] and the production of original work.

Creative people also display a belief that learning is incremental. Their quest for finding better ways of doing things is infinite, and they constantly increase their knowledge and their sophistication in using, adapting and applying that knowledge. The public library system implicitly and explicitly recognises that learning is a process that has no end. The underlying ethos of public libraries, there from the very beginning, is that reading helps us all to become better people with more fulfilled lives. Libraries can, and in many places do, provide platforms for development, or staging posts, to assist young people on their journey. Bookstart, library cards and book packs for the newborn, links to Sure Start, homework clubs, teenage reading groups, and help with becoming proficient in IT are just some of the examples of the ways in which libraries can develop broad reading skills.

A further attitudinal characteristic of creative thinkers is their *enjoyment* of learning. OECD research shows that while young people's literacy in the UK is improving (indeed British children are highly literate by international standards, seventh out of 31 countries in an OECD survey in 2001) large numbers do not read for pleasure – 36 per cent of boys and 22 per cent of girls said that they never read for enjoyment (the OECD averages are 40 per cent for boys, 13 per cent for girls).[17]

Public libraries provide reading for fun, not just material to help pass exams, and reading for pleasure is important:

> *It is not clear to what extent reading for enjoyment leads to higher reading literacy, or the other way round, or to what extent some other aspect of students' background*

contributes to both. Nevertheless, the association between engaging in reading and being good at it is an important one, indicating that it may be productive to encourage both'.[18]

A recent statement by the Secretary of State for Education, announcing funding for the national library programmes Summer Reading Challenge and Orange Chatterbooks, welcomes attempts to increase the enjoyment of reading and sees these programmes as part of 'our wider campaign to cultivate children's enjoyment of reading and writing and to promote creativity across the whole curriculum'.[19]

Motivation

In addition to factors of cognition, knowledge and attitudes, motivation plays a part in the achievement of creativity. Creative work is hard work and requires persistence. Reading is one of few areas of contemporary life (sport and music are others) where young people voluntarily apply themselves in depth and over time. Many have commented on the recent phenomenon of children reading blockbuster novels in one sitting, although there is nothing new in this. Reading seems always to have captivated some children, from those who read the whole of the Biggles series to those who now read Philip Pullman.

Motivation can be improved through people feeling in control of things and from their gaining a sense of achievement. Libraries can help with both. Involving young people in stock selection and display provides a sense of involvement and, as the Chartered Institute of Library and Information Professionals (CILIP) report *Start with the Child* notes, young people have 'a desire to be listened to and offered the chance to contribute ideas...and to exercise a degree of power over their environment'.[20]

The Summer Reading Challenge is an example of a programme that encourages autonomy (readers select their own pace and range) and the sense of achievement born of attaining a goal through application. It also generates 35,000 new library members each year. Homework clubs similarly help young people to work and to achieve.

Creative acts and creative people exist within a context. New ideas and new things have to gain acceptance. For this to happen the outcome of the creative process must be communicated to and valued by others. Creative people thus have to have the ability and above all the confidence to communicate their innovations to others. If ideas are to be adopted they need to be accepted by some (even when challenged by others), particularly by peer groups.

There is growing evidence that libraries' work with young people can affect all these areas: cognition, knowledge, attitudes, motivation and confidence. Evaluations of a number of programmes, notably Reading the Game, Chatterbooks, YouthBOOX, Summer Reading Challenge and Young Cultural Creators, contain case studies demonstrating changes in confidence and motivation. So does research undertaken in 2001 by the University of Surrey.[21] The recently methodology and toolkit created by the Museums, Libraries and Archives Council (MLA), *Inspiring Learning for All*[22], should help to extend and strengthen the evidence over time. The generic learning outcomes looked for in that framework include 'creativity, attitudes and values'. With this new way of assessing and capturing the 'soft' outcomes of their work, libraries should be able to make a strong case for their role in the creativity agenda.

4. Nurturing creativity

Public libraries are rich in resources and potential. There are three fundamental characteristics unique to public libraries that act as the foundations for building a creative reading nation:

○ Public libraries are ubiquitous – there are 3,949 library sites and 655 mobile libraries.
○ Public libraries are free.
○ Public libraries are widely trusted; for example, they are used by 61 per cent of Asian or British Asian, and 57 per cent of Black or British Black people aged 16–44.[23]

But beyond these basic features, the points of correspondence between the activities of public libraries and the development of creative thinking are many.

Library space

First, there is the library space, not just a physical space but a mental and psychological space. A frequent criticism of public libraries is that the condition of buildings leaves much to be desired.[24] Although this is not universally true – there are many examples of fine new or refurbished buildings – and although much is being done to improve matters, it remains the case that many people do not see libraries as physically attractive places. In terms of creativity, libraries need a variety of spaces. Areas of quiet are required: 'The biggest demand in public libraries over the past decade has been for quiet, secure study space'[25] but so are areas of visual and aural stimulus. It would be good to have places in all public libraries where ideas can be recorded with white boards, flipcharts, pens and paper, computer discs and tape recorders.

Public libraries can offer 'raw' space to help the

creativity agenda. For example, Creative Partnerships in Kent is working inside a theatre space in Dover library. They can also link with other creative resources, as in the case of Hampshire's Discovery Centres.[26]

CILIP's report *Start with the Child* highlights the need for 'spaces which support diverse activities and provide a haven for users of different ages'[27], but the report also emphasises young people's 'tendency to become increasingly consumerist and materialistic at a younger age'. In terms of stimulating, creative spaces, we can expect young people to be demanding. They are used to commercial spaces with high standards of finish and regular refits.

The psychological space that public libraries provide to young people in terms of creativity is especially valuable. Neither home nor school, neither shop nor street, it offers millions of young people a safe place for informal, self-directed activity. The intellectual exercise available is playful or rigorous by choice. When young people are in libraries they are not told what to read or what to choose. There are no demands of the curriculum and no exams to be passed. In this sense libraries can provide a relaxed space. But the space should not be neutral or anaemic. Rather it is a positive place where mental comfort and challenge are both available. A place in other words that corresponds with the creative needs of stimulation and reflection, a place that encourages exploration and intellectual risk.

The special niche that public libraries can occupy in young people's lives should not be underestimated. The challenge is to maintain libraries' difference and distinct features while making connections with other aspects of young people's lives and enabling them to make the most of what's on offer. Librarians need to encourage young people's exploration without imposing their own ideas, and libraries need to work in partnership with schools, youth services and social services while maintaining their own sense of identity. It is, and will continue to be, a difficult balancing act.

The personalised approach

Second, there is the importance of the personalised, individual approach. In a world of mass provision and standardised services, libraries are very much tailored to the needs of the individual and, as was noted earlier, the stimulation of creativity is an individual phenomenon. Young people given identical experiences will react differently. The creativity of one may be stimulated by science, of another by music. Librarians have the opportunity to advise and guide library users by starting from the existing interests of the reader. A young person's interest in anything from fishing to hip-hop can be deepened and widened with sympathetic advice. The engagement may come through magazines or CDs in the library – it doesn't matter – but once started the connections can lead anywhere and result in an autonomous, engaged, creative reader.

The benefit of using the reader's interests as a starting point applies not only to the content of the interest, but also to the means of access with which the reader is most comfortable. Public libraries have recognised the importance of IT, and the ability of libraries to offer free computing and web time to young people is now one of their greatest strengths.

The YouthBOOX programme offers a model of how reading can be encouraged using the particular interests of individuals as a starting point. Their principle of 'start with the reader' has enabled the programme to bring into libraries young people who otherwise would never have crossed the threshold.

Creative spaces

Third, libraries are the locus of a number of programmes specifically allied to the creativity agenda where young people undertake creative activity themselves and are stimulated by contact with creative professionals. These programmes include:

o   Young Cultural Creators – a library-led visual literacy project that links libraries with schools, brings children into libraries, museums and galleries to meet authors, and encourages them to produce their own creative work.

○ Creative Partnerships – a close working partnership developed between Creative Partnerships in Slough and Slough public library, using graphic novels as a way into developing creative work, and resulting in more children using their local library.

○ Books Connect – a library led, cross-domain programme that uses reading as a launch pad for creative activity expressed through the arts; it combines reading with the creative resources of museums and archives.

○ YouthBOOX – a project where reluctant readers are shown that reading can be empowering, relevant to their lives, and fun; it promotes creativity through the production of videos, cartoons, magazine writing and theatre trips among other things.

(Further information about these programmes can be found on their websites listed in the bibliography.)

An experience of the creative world

Fourth, many libraries work with creative professionals in order to provide children with a rich experience of the world of creativity. Storytellers, authors, illustrators and actors are all involved working with children inside public libraries.

Given the number and variety of the creative activities going on in libraries, they should be seen as one of the primary means by which the government can fulfil the cultural pledge given in the green paper *The Next Ten Years*: 'We want to give a cultural pledge so that, in time, every pupil will have the chance to work with creative professionals and organisations and thereby to enrich their learning'.[28]

5. Public libraries and schools

Every child has the right to read and write creatively and we believe that creativity should become a central part of formal education. All children should have a treasure trove of references, keepsakes, diversions and enrichments – touchstones which will be a source of inspiration for life.

Booktrust[29]

There is a lack of co-operation across public libraries, libraries in schools and school library services.

CILIP[30]

Many of the people interviewed for this project pondered on how public libraries, school libraries and school library services could best coordinate their efforts in relation to young people's creativity. As Sarah McNicol comments, 'school and public libraries…have different emphases for their work. This means that there are likely to be benefits for both in collaborating and drawing on each other's strengths'.[31]

Given the need for individual responses to and routes into creativity, it seems that the various elements should offer a variety of complementary but coordinated responses. All school libraries, for example, should contain imaginative fiction, poetry and non-fiction relevant to young people's lives and interests, extending beyond the needs of the curriculum. Teachers should be active advocates of public libraries to their pupils, and should know their local librarians. Public libraries in turn need to make schools aware of what they can offer. More impact research is needed on how good school libraries, and partnerships between public libraries and schools, can improve creative capacity.

One area of particular strength of public libraries in relation to formal education is their 'backlist'. The range of material that they can offer to young people will always be greater than that available in school libraries or in bookshops, though it must be swiftly and easily accessible if it is to be of use. Teachers need to know how libraries can extend and deepen the learning that takes place in schools, and should use the expertise of librarians who are best placed to navigate the learning resources that they are responsible for.

Supporting learning in schools

There are many ways in which public libraries support learning in schools – through the way that librarians help children find materials for projects to homework clubs. Libraries can play a particular role in making the curriculum come alive. Historical romances can illuminate a young person's understanding of history and libraries can provide biographies of musicians, for example. It is these kinds of exploration that broaden and deepen understanding and demonstrate the connectivity of knowledge that is so vital in creative thinking. Charles Clarke's endorsement for pleasure in reading is further strengthened by Ofsted's recent inspections relating to wider reading and reading for pleasure, which give schools the validation for joint working with libraries.

Framework for the Future notes that 'Many library services are developing closer relationships with school age children to support the work of schools',[32] and there is an obvious need for professionals in schools, public libraries and school library services to work together to support the creativity of young people. In some areas this is already happening, with strong links and working relationships established between the various parties (joint school and public library book-buying trips for example), but in others the connections are less well established. It seems clear, however, that the relationships develop differently from place to place, and that providing hard and fast definitions of the roles of the different partners would be likely to be counterproductive. Cooperation and partnership working need themselves to be creative activities.

There is nothing wrong with differing models of practice, or with blurred boundaries between roles, but in order to work well, professional barriers and professional mystique need to be abandoned.

Effective partnerships are productive, yet at the same time it is vital that when public libraries are working with others they do not lose their special status as sites of informal, autonomous learning. As creative spaces they need to maintain a separate identity for exploratory freedom, a space distinct from the formal education system.

6. Conclusion

Reading is a creative activity in and of itself. It encourages connections and provides stimulus. It links to other types of cultural expression and other art forms. It helps young people to explore the world and enriches them educationally and emotionally.

By providing free access to reading, public libraries play a unique and important role in the development of a creative nation. Public libraries can provide many of the ingredients for creative exploration, including stimulus, knowledge, self-directed activity, zones of freedom away from the structures of home and school, links to communities of interest via clubs and the web, and putting enjoyment and pleasure into reading and learning.

But there are challenges in making the most of

what public libraries can offer young people in terms of developing their creativity. Many of these issues are well known and apply at a more general level: opening hours, local variations in service and the lack of a national quality framework, badly located buildings in poor repair, joining procedures, problems with stock and questions of how to bring in non-users. These are all well documented[33] and in parts of the country action is being taken to make beneficial changes. The approaches taken in some of the national library programmes that relate to creativity in fact help with these issues. Giving young people a creative role in stock selection, engaging with them by starting from their own interests, doing outreach work with schools and creative professionals all help to build a better library service as well as to encourage young people's creativity.

There is also a set of wider systemic and societal issues that affect the ability of young people to use libraries freely: parental fear of allowing their children to make the journey to libraries alone, problems with transport, out-of-town shopping moving the focus of the family weekend away from town centres. Fewer children can walk or cycle by themselves to a local branch library than in the past. Paradoxically, while library buildings are getting better, the stock of children's books is much improved and specialist children's librarians can be found in many places, it can be harder for children, particularly children whose parents have no interest in taking them to the library, to gain access to these improvements. Libraries cannot control these factors, but they can adapt to meet the challenge, for example through outreach work and changing opening hours.

In relation to creativity, the particular issues are:

○ When bringing buildings up to the best standards, attention needs to be paid to creating a variety of spaces to reflect different user needs and desires.

○ New-build and refurbished libraries should make connections with other creative resources both in the public sector – such as being located near archives, museums, arts centres or theatres – and in the private sector, where libraries can be part of 'creative clusters'.

O The furnishing and layout of libraries should take account of the creative process, providing stimulus, surprise, random connections and different means of recording ideas.

O Stock selection and display should be a conversational process taking into account the wishes of young people, the needs of teachers and the professionalism of librarians. The result should be stock that stretches the imagination and opens up new possibilities. Librarians should take risks in selecting periodicals and book stock and be adventurous with display and arrangement.

O Schools, homes and public libraries

need to be linked in a virtuous circle without losing libraries' difference and distinction.

O   Young people should be involved not only in stock selection and library design, but can play a role on the front line and behind the scenes in public libraries. Public libraries should offer work experience, volunteer schemes, and adopt recruitment procedures to stimulate this.

O   Library staff need to understand their role in the creativity agenda, have confidence that they are part of the creative world and determine strategies to engage with creativity.

O   *All* young people, not just some, should be given the opportunity to engage with creativity through programmes and activities offered in a library context.

O   Policy-makers and libraries need to work together to determine libraries'

role in the emerging debate about
cultural entitlement.

○ Teachers and others in the formal
education sector need to understand
the benefits of working with public
libraries on the creativity agenda and
to make young people that they teach
aware of what public libraries offer.
School library services can play a
powerful bridging and brokering role
in building school–public library
partnerships.

○ Continuous investment in ICT will be
needed in order to keep libraries' offer
to young people current and fresh.

Relevant websites

www.artsandlibraries.org.uk
www.booktrust.org.uk,
www.branching-out.org.uk
www.creative-partnerships.com
www.inspiringlearningforall.gov.uk
www.mla.gov.uk
www.pisa.oecd.org
www.readingagency.org.uk (also for
Booksconnect and YouthBOOX)
www.readingmaze.org.uk
www.whatareyouuptotonight.com
www.youngculturalcreators.com

Notes

1. BML, *Reading the Situation: Book reading, buying and borrowing habits in Britain* (Book Marketing Ltd and The Reading Agency, 2000).
2. DCMS, *Framework for the Future: Libraries, learning and information in the next decade* (Department for Culture, Media and Sport, 2003).
3. OECD, 'What PISA tells us' (OECD, 2001). Available at www.pisa.oecd.org/knowledge/summary/e.htm.
4. S R Fischer, *A History of Reading* (Reaktion, 2003).
5. S Appleyard, *Becoming a Reader: the experience of fiction from childhood to adulthood* (Cambridge University Press, 1991).
6. R W Emerson, *The American Scholar* (1837), quoted in A Manguel, *A History of Reading* (Flamingo, 1996).
7. NACCCE, *All Our Futures: Creativity, culture and education* (National Advisory Committee on Creative and Cultural Education, 2000).
8. DCMS, *The Next Ten Years: Culture and creativity*(Department for Culture, Media and Sport, 2001).
9. NACCE, *All Our Futures*.
10. Speech by Charles Clarke, 3 June 2003.

11. Building Futures, *21st Century Libraries: Changing forms, changing futures* (Building Futures, 2004).
12. Ofsted, *Expecting the Unexpected: Developing creativity in primary and secondary schools* (Office for Standards in Education, 2003).
13. M Csikszentmihalyi, *Flow* (Random House, 2002).
14. A J Cropley, *Creativity in Education and Learning:A guide for teachers and educators* (Kegan Page Ltd, 2001).
15. DCMS, *Framework for the Future*.
16. OECD Programme for International Student Assessment (PISA), 'Reading literacy' in *The PISA 2003 Assessment Framework: Mathematics, Reading, Science and Problem-Solving Knowledge and Skills* (OECD, 2004).
17. OECD, 'What PISA tells us'.
18. Ibid.
19. Statement by Charles Clarke at Museums, Libraries and Archives Council conference, 2 March 2004.
20. CILIP, *Start with the Child* (Chartered Institute of Library and Information Professionals, 2002).
21. MLA press release 'Libraries lead the way in inspiring children to read', 9 July 2003.
22. Available from www.inspiringlearningforall.gov.uk/ utilities/download_library/index.aspx.
23. ACE, *Focus on Cultural Diversity: the arts in England – attendance, participation and attitudes* (Arts Council England, 2003).
24. CABE, *Better Public Libraries* (Commission for Architecture and the Built Environment, Museums, Libraries and Archives Council, 2003).

25. Building Futures, *21st Century Libraries*.
26. Hampshire County Council leaflet 'Introducing the Discovery Centre Concept' (Hampshire County Council, 2002).
27. CILIP, *Start with the Child*.
28. DCMS, *The Next Ten Years*.
29. Booktrust, 'Writing together: literature entitlement' (2004). Available to download from www.booktrust.org.uk.
30. CILIP, *Start with the Child*.
31. S McNicol, *Reader Development and Reading Promotion in School Libraries and Public Libraries* (Isle of Wight Council, 2003).
32. DCMS, *Framework for the Future*.
33. Ibid. See also C Leadbeater, *Overdue: How to create a modern public library service* (Demos, 2003), and T Coates, *Who's in Charge? Responsibility for the public library service* (LIBRI, 2004).

DEMOS – Licence to Publish

THE WORK (AS DEFINED BELOW) IS PROVIDED UNDER THE TERMS OF THIS LICENCE ("LICENCE"). THE WORK IS PROTECTED BY COPYRIGHT AND/OR OTHER APPLICABLE LAW. ANY USE OF THE WORK OTHER THAN AS AUTHORIZED UNDER THIS LICENCE IS PROHIBITED. BY EXERCISING ANY RIGHTS TO THE WORK PROVIDED HERE, YOU ACCEPT AND AGREE TO BE BOUND BY THE TERMS OF THIS LICENCE. DEMOS GRANTS YOU THE RIGHTS CONTAINED HERE IN CONSIDERATION OF YOUR ACCEPTANCE OF SUCH TERMS AND CONDITIONS.

1. **Definitions**
   a   **"Collective Work"** means a work, such as a periodical issue, anthology or encyclopedia, in which the Work in its entirety in unmodified form, along with a number of other contributions, constituting separate and independent works in themselves, are assembled into a collective whole. A work that constitutes a Collective Work will not be considered a Derivative Work (as defined below) for the purposes of this Licence.
   b   **"Derivative Work"** means a work based upon the Work or upon the Work and other pre-existing works, such as a musical arrangement, dramatization, fictionalization, motion picture version, sound recording, art reproduction, abridgment, condensation, or any other form in which the Work may be recast, transformed, or adapted, except that a work that constitutes a Collective Work or a translation from English into another language will not be considered a Derivative Work for the purpose of this Licence.
   c   **"Licensor"** means the individual or entity that offers the Work under the terms of this Licence.
   d   **"Original Author"** means the individual or entity who created the Work.
   e   **"Work"** means the copyrightable work of authorship offered under the terms of this Licence.
   f   **"You"** means an individual or entity exercising rights under this Licence who has not previously violated the terms of this Licence with respect to the Work, or who has received express permission from DEMOS to exercise rights under this Licence despite a previous violation.

2. **Fair Use Rights.** Nothing in this licence is intended to reduce, limit, or restrict any rights arising from fair use, first sale or other limitations on the exclusive rights of the copyright owner under copyright law or other applicable laws.

3. **Licence Grant.** Subject to the terms and conditions of this Licence, Licensor hereby grants You a worldwide, royalty-free, non-exclusive, perpetual (for the duration of the applicable copyright) licence to exercise the rights in the Work as stated below:

   a to reproduce the Work, to incorporate the Work into one or more Collective Works, and to reproduce the Work as incorporated in the Collective Works;

   b to distribute copies or phonorecords of, display publicly, perform publicly, and perform publicly by means of a digital audio transmission the Work including as incorporated in Collective Works;

   The above rights may be exercised in all media and formats whether now known or hereafter devised. The above rights include the right to make such modifications as are technically necessary to exercise the rights in other media and formats. All rights not expressly granted by Licensor are hereby reserved.

4. **Restrictions.** The licence granted in Section 3 above is expressly made subject to and limited by the following restrictions:

   a You may distribute, publicly display, publicly perform, or publicly digitally perform the Work only under the terms of this Licence, and You must include a copy of, or the Uniform Resource Identifier for, this Licence with every copy or phonorecord of the Work You distribute, publicly display, publicly perform, or publicly digitally perform. You may not offer or impose any terms on the Work that alter or restrict the terms of this Licence or the recipients' exercise of the rights granted hereunder. You may not sublicence the Work. You must keep intact all notices that refer to this Licence and to the disclaimer of warranties. You may not distribute, publicly display, publicly perform, or publicly digitally perform the Work with any technological measures that control access or use of the Work in a manner inconsistent with the terms of this Licence Agreement. The above applies to the Work as incorporated in a Collective Work, but this does not require the Collective Work apart from the Work itself to be made subject to the terms of this Licence. If You create a Collective Work, upon notice from any Licencor You must, to the extent practicable, remove from the Collective Work any reference to such Licensor or the Original Author, as requested.

b You may not exercise any of the rights granted to You in Section 3 above in any manner that is primarily intended for or directed toward commercial advantage or private monetary compensation. The exchange of the Work for other copyrighted works by means of digital file-sharing or otherwise shall not be considered to be intended for or directed toward commercial advantage or private monetary compensation, provided there is no payment of any monetary compensation in connection with the exchange of copyrighted works.

c If you distribute, publicly display, publicly perform, or publicly digitally perform the Work or any Collective Works, You must keep intact all copyright notices for the Work and give the Original Author credit reasonable to the medium or means You are utilizing by conveying the name (or pseudonym if applicable) of the Original Author if supplied; the title of the Work if supplied. Such credit may be implemented in any reasonable manner; provided, however, that in the case of a Collective Work, at a minimum such credit will appear where any other comparable authorship credit appears and in a manner at least as prominent as such other comparable authorship credit.

5. Representations, Warranties and Disclaimer

a By offering the Work for public release under this Licence, Licensor represents and warrants that, to the best of Licensor's knowledge after reasonable inquiry:

i Licensor has secured all rights in the Work necessary to grant the licence rights hereunder and to permit the lawful exercise of the rights granted hereunder without You having any obligation to pay any royalties, compulsory licence fees, residuals or any other payments;

ii The Work does not infringe the copyright, trademark, publicity rights, common law rights or any other right of any third party or constitute defamation, invasion of privacy or other tortious injury to any third party.

b EXCEPT AS EXPRESSLY STATED IN THIS LICENCE OR OTHERWISE AGREED IN WRITING OR REQUIRED BY APPLICABLE LAW, THE WORK IS LICENCED ON AN "AS IS" BASIS, WITHOUT WARRANTIES OF ANY KIND, EITHER EXPRESS OR IMPLIED INCLUDING, WITHOUT LIMITATION, ANY WARRANTIES REGARDING THE CONTENTS OR ACCURACY OF THE WORK.

6. **Limitation on Liability.** EXCEPT TO THE EXTENT REQUIRED BY APPLICABLE LAW, AND EXCEPT FOR DAMAGES ARISING FROM LIABILITY TO A THIRD PARTY RESULTING FROM BREACH OF THE WARRANTIES IN SECTION 5, IN NO EVENT WILL LICENSOR BE LIABLE TO YOU ON ANY LEGAL THEORY FOR ANY SPECIAL, INCIDENTAL, CONSEQUENTIAL, PUNITIVE OR EXEMPLARY DAMAGES ARISING OUT OF THIS LICENCE OR THE USE OF THE WORK, EVEN IF LICENSOR HAS BEEN ADVISED OF THE POSSIBILITY OF SUCH DAMAGES.

7. **Termination**
   a This Licence and the rights granted hereunder will terminate automatically upon any breach by You of the terms of this Licence. Individuals or entities who have received Collective Works from You under this Licence, however, will not have their licences terminated provided such individuals or entities remain in full compliance with those licences. Sections 1, 2, 5, 6, 7, and 8 will survive any termination of this Licence.
   b Subject to the above terms and conditions, the licence granted here is perpetual (for the duration of the applicable copyright in the Work). Notwithstanding the above, Licensor reserves the right to release the Work under different licence terms or to stop distributing the Work at any time; provided, however that any such election will not serve to withdraw this Licence (or any other licence that has been, or is required to be, granted under the terms of this Licence), and this Licence will continue in full force and effect unless terminated as stated above.

8. Miscellaneous
   a Each time You distribute or publicly digitally perform the Work or a Collective Work, DEMOS offers to the recipient a licence to the Work on the same terms and conditions as the licence granted to You under this Licence.
   b If any provision of this Licence is invalid or unenforceable under applicable law, it shall not affect the validity or enforceability of the remainder of the terms of this Licence, and without further action by the parties to this agreement, such provision shall be reformed to the minimum extent necessary to make such provision valid and enforceable.
   c No term or provision of this Licence shall be deemed waived and no breach consented to unless such waiver or consent shall be in writing and signed by the party to be charged with such waiver or consent.

Copyright

d This Licence constitutes the entire agreement between the parties with respect to the Work licensed here. There are no understandings, agreements or representations with respect to the Work not specified here. Licensor shall not be bound by any additional provisions that may appear in any communication from You. This Licence may not be modified without the mutual written agreement of DEMOS and You.